I love reading

by Mon...

Editorial consultant: Mitch Cronick

We would like to thank: Shirley Bickler and Suzanne Baker

ISBN 1 86007 971 7 pbk
Printed in China

Picture credits
t=top, b=bottom, c=centre, l-left, r=right, OFC= outside front cover
FLPA: 18-19. Shutterstock: 10-11, 14, 20t. Superstock: OFC, 7, 8, 15, 16-17.
ticktock photography: OFC, 4, 5, 6, 12, 13, 14-15c, 20b, 21.

CONTENTS

3

Meet the snakes

Snakes have a scaly skin.

The skin feels dry.

Scaly skin

Snakes sleep with their eyes open.

Snakes have a tongue. It looks like a Y.

5

Snake babies

Some snakes lay eggs.

They lay eggs in nests.

Corn snake

Baby snakes hatch from the eggs.

Some snakes do not lay eggs.

They have baby snakes.

Anaconda snake

8

Scaly skin

King cobra

The king cobra is poisonous.

It is the biggest poisonous snake.

The king cobra hunts for birds and rats.

It spits poison at them.

The king cobra lays eggs.

9

Adder

The adder is a poisonous snake too.

It eats rats and lizards.

The adder has baby snakes.

It can have 20 baby snakes at one time.

Royal python

This snake eats rats and gerbils.

It grabs the animals.

It wraps its body around them.

Then it squeezes all the air out of them and eats them.

Rattlesnake

The rattlesnake hunts for rats and mice.

Its fangs are poisonous.

It bites the rats and mice to kill them.

Then it eats them.

Fangs

It has hard scales on its tail.

The hard scales rattle.

The rattlesnake does not lay eggs.
It has baby snakes.

Tongue like a Y

Anaconda

The anaconda eats pigs and deer.

It wraps its body around the animals.

Then it squeezes them to death.

Anaconda

16

Tongue like a Y

The anaconda does not lay eggs.

It has baby snakes.

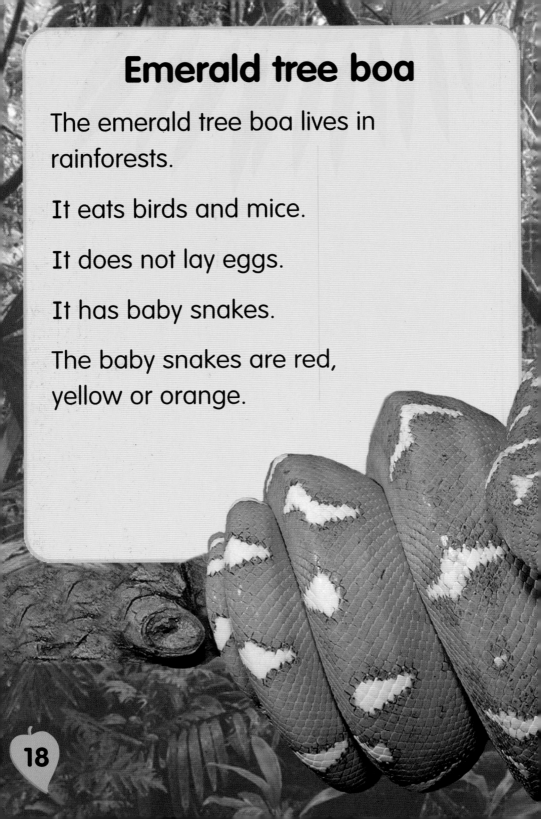

Emerald tree boa

The emerald tree boa lives in rainforests.

It eats birds and mice.

It does not lay eggs.

It has baby snakes.

The baby snakes are red, yellow or orange.

Baby emerald tree boa

Corn snake

This snake is not poisonous.

A corn snake makes a good pet.

It is not scary!

It eats rats and mice.

Tongue like a Y

It lives in trees and under rocks.

The corn snake lays its eggs in old leaves.

Scaly skin

What? Which? How?

What do all snakes have?

- **Scaly skin**
- **Tongue like a Y**
- **Poisonous fangs**

Which snake lives in the rainforest?

- **Rattlesnake**
- **Anaconda**
- **Emerald tree boa**

What do these snakes eat?

- **Emerald tree boa**
- **Anaconda**
- **Corn snake**

How do these snakes catch their food?

- **Anaconda**
- **King cobra**
- **Royal python**

Which snake do you think is the most scary? Why?

Activities

What did you think of this book?

 Brilliant   **Good**    **OK**

Which page did you like best? Why?

• • • • • • • • • • • • •

Which snakes eat these animals?

rats • birds • deer

• • • • • • • • • • • • •

Which is the odd one out? Why?

adder • corn snake • rattlesnake

• • • • • • • • • • • • •

Who is the author of this book?
Have you read *Bug Watch* by the same author?